MONET'S

ADDRESS BOOK

Abbeville Press • Publishers

Cover: **FREDERICK FRIESEKE** *(1874-1939).* **The Garden Parasol,** *c.1909.*
Oil on canvas, 57 x 76⅝ in. (144.8 x 194.6 cm). North Carolina Museum of Art, Raleigh.

Title page: **GUY ROSE** *(1867-1925).* **The Blue Kimono,** *c. 1909.*
Oil on canvas, 31 x 19 in. (78.7 x 48.3 cm). Terry and Paula Trotter; Trotter Galleries.

Based on **Monet's Giverny: An Impressionist Colony** *by William H. Gerdts, published by Abbeville Press, 1993.*

Copyright © 1994 by Abbeville Press, Inc. All rights reserved under international copyright conventions. No part of this work may be reproduced or utilized in any form or by any means, electronic or mechanical, including photocopying, recording, or by any information storage and retrieval system, without permission in writing from the publisher. Inquiries should be addressed to Abbeville Publishing Group, 488 Madison Avenue, New York, NY 10022. Printed in Hong Kong.
ISBN 1-55859-769-7

CLAUDE MONET (1840–1926). *In the Woods at Giverny; Blanche Hoschedé-Monet at Her Easel with Suzanne Hoschedé Reading,* 1887.
Oil on canvas, 36 x 38½ in. Los Angeles County Museum of Art; Mr. and Mrs. George Gard De Sylva Collection.

Family members, such as his step-daughters depicted here, served as Monet's models for the figure studies he worked on during the late 1880s. Capturing figures in a landscape allowed Monet to experiment with both composition and color; here he carefully balances the women, the easel, and the trees against a sparkling background of various greens and hints of light blue. Sunlight seems to seep in from the sides of the painting, illuminating the sitters' gowns with subtle strokes of yellow and purple-blue.

LILLA CABOT PERRY (1848–1933). *Child Sewing at a Window*, n.d.
Oil on canvas mounted on Masonite, 21¾ x 18 1/4 in. Private collection.

Perry and her husband were instrumental in popularizing both Monet's work and Impressionism in the United States. She and her family spent numerous summers at Giverny, where the American painter was among the handful of artists who became close to Monet. Perry divided her efforts between figure and landscape images, which allowed her to investigate the still-radical Impressionist aesthetic while continuing to work, at times, in a more academic style. In figural studies such as this one, she maintained firm structure through sure drawing, tonal modeling, and strong contrasts of light and shade; the only bright color is the vivid red of the child's sewing material.

A

Name _____ *Phone* _____
Address _____
City & State _____ *Zip* _____ *Birthday* _____

Name _____ *Phone* _____
Address _____
City & State _____ *Zip* _____ *Birthday* _____

Name _____ *Phone* _____
Address _____
City & State _____ *Zip* _____ *Birthday* _____

Name _____ *Phone* _____
Address _____
City & State _____ *Zip* _____ *Birthday* _____

Name _____ *Phone* _____
Address _____
City & State _____ *Zip* _____ *Birthday* _____

Name _____ *Phone* _____
Address _____
City & State _____ *Zip* _____ *Birthday* _____

Name _____ *Phone* _____
Address _____
City & State _____ *Zip* _____ *Birthday* _____

Name _____ *Phone* _____
Address _____
City & State _____ *Zip* _____ *Birthday* _____

Name		Phone	
Address			
City & State	Zip	Birthday	

Name		Phone	
Address			
City & State	Zip	Birthday	

Name		Phone	
Address			
City & State	Zip	Birthday	

Name		Phone	
Address			
City & State	Zip	Birthday	

Name		Phone	
Address			
City & State	Zip	Birthday	

Name		Phone	
Address			
City & State	Zip	Birthday	

Name		Phone	
Address			
City & State	Zip	Birthday	

Name		Phone	
Address			
City & State	Zip	Birthday	

Name	*Phone*
Address	
City & State / *Zip*	*Birthday*

Name	*Phone*
Address	
City & State / *Zip*	*Birthday*

Name	*Phone*
Address	
City & State / *Zip*	*Birthday*

Name	*Phone*
Address	
City & State / *Zip*	*Birthday*

Name	*Phone*
Address	
City & State / *Zip*	*Birthday*

Name	*Phone*
Address	
City & State / *Zip*	*Birthday*

Name	*Phone*
Address	
City & State / *Zip*	*Birthday*

Name	*Phone*
Address	
City & State / *Zip*	*Birthday*

Name		Phone	
Address			
City & State	Zip	Birthday	

Name		Phone	
Address			
City & State	Zip	Birthday	

Name		Phone	
Address			
City & State	Zip	Birthday	

Name		Phone	
Address			
City & State	Zip	Birthday	

Name		Phone	
Address			
City & State	Zip	Birthday	

Name		Phone	
Address			
City & State	Zip	Birthday	

Name		Phone	
Address			
City & State	Zip	Birthday	

Name		Phone	
Address			
City & State	Zip	Birthday	

FREDERICK FRIESEKE (1874–1939). *Lady in a Garden*, c. 1912.
Oil on canvas, 31⅞ x 25¾ in. Daniel J. Terra Collection.

Frederick Frieseke was the dominant figure among the third generation of artists in Giverny, a group whose work became increasingly decorative and more concerned with overall pattern than with reproducing nature's tones. **Lady in a Garden** is Frieseke's vibrant version of a typical Giverny theme: the contemplative young woman in a sun-drenched, enclosed garden, the symbolic safe haven for female purity. The scene is a study in strong color and decorative pattern; the bold stripes on the woman's dress allows her to blend into the multitude of flowers around her, creating an almost two-dimensional image.

LOUIS RITTER (1854–1892). *Flowers: Peonies and Snowballs,* 1887.
Oil on canvas, 39⅜ x 32⁵⁄₁₆ in. Terra Foundation for the Arts; Daniel J. Terra Collection.

A student in Munich during the early 1880s, Ritter abandoned the dark, dramatic manner that informed his early work when he came to Giverny in 1887, but continued to resist fully adopting Impressionist techniques. In this beautiful still life—a rare example of a conventional indoor floral piece among artists dedicated to plein-air painting—Ritter uses vivid colors, but the forms of the petals, leaves, and vase are carefully rendered rather than dissolved in light and atmosphere, as they would be in a purely Impressionist work.

B

Name _____ *Phone* _____
Address _____
City & State _____ *Zip* _____ *Birthday* _____

Name _____ *Phone* _____
Address _____
City & State _____ *Zip* _____ *Birthday* _____

Name _____ *Phone* _____
Address _____
City & State _____ *Zip* _____ *Birthday* _____

Name _____ *Phone* _____
Address _____
City & State _____ *Zip* _____ *Birthday* _____

Name _____ *Phone* _____
Address _____
City & State _____ *Zip* _____ *Birthday* _____

Name _____ *Phone* _____
Address _____
City & State _____ *Zip* _____ *Birthday* _____

Name _____ *Phone* _____
Address _____
City & State _____ *Zip* _____ *Birthday* _____

Name _____ *Phone* _____
Address _____
City & State _____ *Zip* _____ *Birthday* _____

Name		Phone	
Address			
City & State	Zip	Birthday	

Name		Phone	
Address			
City & State	Zip	Birthday	

Name		Phone	
Address			
City & State	Zip	Birthday	

Name		Phone	
Address			
City & State	Zip	Birthday	

Name		Phone	
Address			
City & State	Zip	Birthday	

Name		Phone	
Address			
City & State	Zip	Birthday	

Name		Phone	
Address			
City & State	Zip	Birthday	

Name		Phone	
Address			
City & State	Zip	Birthday	

Name _____ *Phone* _____

Address _____

City & State _____ *Zip* _____ *Birthday* _____

Name _____ *Phone* _____

Address _____

City & State _____ *Zip* _____ *Birthday* _____

Name _____ *Phone* _____

Address _____

City & State _____ *Zip* _____ *Birthday* _____

Name _____ *Phone* _____

Address _____

City & State _____ *Zip* _____ *Birthday* _____

Name _____ *Phone* _____

Address _____

City & State _____ *Zip* _____ *Birthday* _____

Name _____ *Phone* _____

Address _____

City & State _____ *Zip* _____ *Birthday* _____

Name _____ *Phone* _____

Address _____

City & State _____ *Zip* _____ *Birthday* _____

Name _____ *Phone* _____

Address _____

City & State _____ *Zip* _____ *Birthday* _____

Name		*Phone*	
Address			
City & State	*Zip*	*Birthday*	

Name _____ *Phone* _____
Address _____
City & State _____ *Zip* _____ *Birthday* _____

Name _____ *Phone* _____
Address _____
City & State _____ *Zip* _____ *Birthday* _____

Name _____ *Phone* _____
Address _____
City & State _____ *Zip* _____ *Birthday* _____

Name _____ *Phone* _____
Address _____
City & State _____ *Zip* _____ *Birthday* _____

Name _____ *Phone* _____
Address _____
City & State _____ *Zip* _____ *Birthday* _____

Name _____ *Phone* _____
Address _____
City & State _____ *Zip* _____ *Birthday* _____

Name _____ *Phone* _____
Address _____
City & State _____ *Zip* _____ *Birthday* _____

Name _____ *Phone* _____
Address _____
City & State _____ *Zip* _____ *Birthday* _____

GUY ROSE (1867–1925). *On the River*, c. 1908.
Oil on canvas, 23¾ x 19 in. Rose Family Collection.

This painting of Sadie Frieseke, the wife of Rose's colleague Frederick Frieseke, illustrates a variation on the figure studies many of the Giverny colonists executed at this time. Rather than portraying the female model in an enclosed garden, the artist shows her on a boat, surrounded by shimmering green and blue water instead of colorful flowers. This image owes little to the influence of Monet (who continued to document the effects of weather patterns on views of landscapes and buildings), except in the loose brushwork and the rendering of light and shadow on the river.

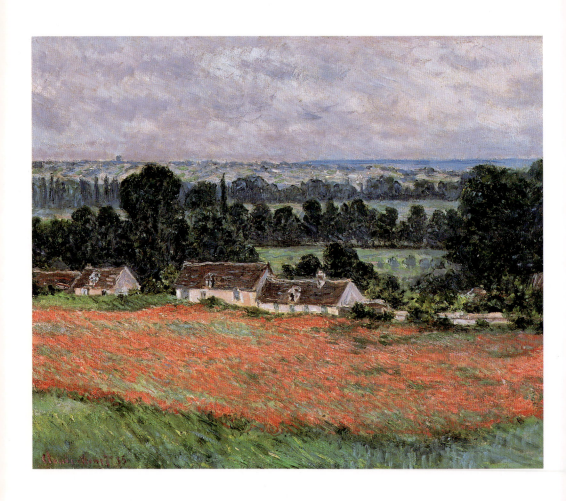

CLAUDE MONET (1840–1926). **Field of Poppies, Giverny,** *1885.*
Oil on canvas, 25⅝ x 28¾ in. Virginia Museum of Fine Arts, Richmond; Collection of Mr. and Mrs. Paul Mellon.

As with the grain stack paintings, Monet created a series of images of poppy fields, a subject matter that was also taken up by the colonists. This bright summer landscape, with its blazing splash of red across the foreground, was shown to great critical acclaim in New York in 1886. Some of the artists who later came to Giverny may well have seen—and been inspired by—this particular painting. The colonists, however, tended to paint more literally than Monet, carefully rendering flowers and greenery rather than allowing the pure, brilliant colors to dissolve into each other.

Name _____ *Phone* _____

Address _____

City & State _____ *Zip* _____ *Birthday* _____

Name _____ *Phone* _____

Address _____

City & State _____ *Zip* _____ *Birthday* _____

Name _____ *Phone* _____

Address _____

City & State _____ *Zip* _____ *Birthday* _____

Name _____ *Phone* _____

Address _____

City & State _____ *Zip* _____ *Birthday* _____

Name _____ *Phone* _____

Address _____

City & State _____ *Zip* _____ *Birthday* _____

Name _____ *Phone* _____

Address _____

City & State _____ *Zip* _____ *Birthday* _____

Name _____ *Phone* _____

Address _____

City & State _____ *Zip* _____ *Birthday* _____

Name _____ *Phone* _____

Address _____

City & State _____ *Zip* _____ *Birthday* _____

Name _____ *Phone* _____
Address _____
City & State _____ *Zip* _____ *Birthday* _____

Name _____ *Phone* _____
Address _____
City & State _____ *Zip* _____ *Birthday* _____

Name _____ *Phone* _____
Address _____
City & State _____ *Zip* _____ *Birthday* _____

Name _____ *Phone* _____
Address _____
City & State _____ *Zip* _____ *Birthday* _____

Name _____ *Phone* _____
Address _____
City & State _____ *Zip* _____ *Birthday* _____

Name _____ *Phone* _____
Address _____
City & State _____ *Zip* _____ *Birthday* _____

Name _____ *Phone* _____
Address _____
City & State _____ *Zip* _____ *Birthday* _____

Name _____ *Phone* _____
Address _____
City & State _____ *Zip* _____ *Birthday* _____

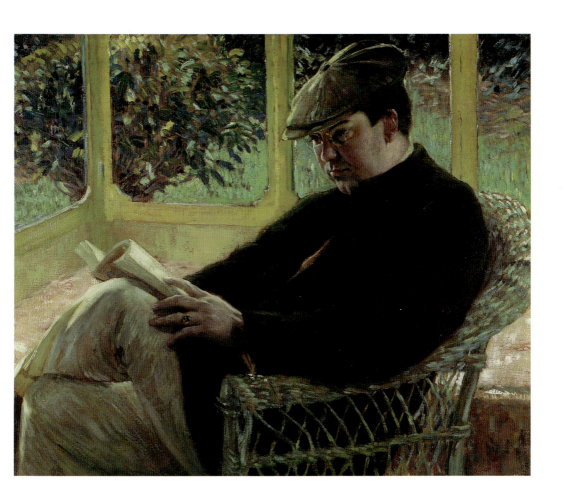

LAWTON S. PARKER (1868–1954). Frederick Frieseke, c. 1913.
Oil on canvas, 25⅝ x 32 in. National Academy of Design, New York.

In Parker's portrait of his friend and mentor, the figure itself is rendered in a fairly traditional, naturalistic manner, while the background illustrates some of the decorative influences he absorbed from Frieseke. The window panes are punctuated with a strong vertical pattern of yellow, and the bush outside appears to be on the same plane as the yellow stripes, creating a unified, decorative backdrop for the portrait.

KARL ALBERT BUEHR (1866–1952). *Picnic on the Grass*, 1911–12.
Oil on canvas, 31½ x 39 in. Private collection; Courtesy of Mongerson-Wunderlich Galleries, Chicago.

German-born Karl Albert Buehr joined the Giverny colony around 1911; he soon became an inspired practicioner of decorative Impressionism. In this depiction of a young woman by the river's edge, the dappled sunlight illuminates the contrast between the glowing orange parasol, the soft purple and white gown, the bright turquoise cloth in the foreground, and the iridescent paleness of the woman's flesh. The figure, and all the elements surrounding her, are defined by the interlocking patterns of colors and brushstrokes, so that the whole image seems to exist on one decorative, pictorial plane.

D

Name _____ *Phone* _____
Address _____
City & State _____ *Zip* _____ *Birthday* _____

Name _____ *Phone* _____
Address _____
City & State _____ *Zip* _____ *Birthday* _____

Name _____ *Phone* _____
Address _____
City & State _____ *Zip* _____ *Birthday* _____

Name _____ *Phone* _____
Address _____
City & State _____ *Zip* _____ *Birthday* _____

Name _____ *Phone* _____
Address _____
City & State _____ *Zip* _____ *Birthday* _____

Name _____ *Phone* _____
Address _____
City & State _____ *Zip* _____ *Birthday* _____

Name _____ *Phone* _____
Address _____
City & State _____ *Zip* _____ *Birthday* _____

Name _____ *Phone* _____
Address _____
City & State _____ *Zip* _____ *Birthday* _____

Name		Phone	
Address			
City & State	Zip	Birthday	

Name		Phone	
Address			
City & State	Zip	Birthday	

Name		Phone	
Address			
City & State	Zip	Birthday	

Name		Phone	
Address			
City & State	Zip	Birthday	

Name		Phone	
Address			
City & State	Zip	Birthday	

Name		Phone	
Address			
City & State	Zip	Birthday	

Name		Phone	
Address			
City & State	Zip	Birthday	

Name		Phone	
Address			
City & State	Zip	Birthday	

Name		Phone	
Address			
City & State	Zip	Birthday	

Name		Phone	
Address			
City & State	Zip	Birthday	

Name		Phone	
Address			
City & State	Zip	Birthday	

Name		Phone	
Address			
City & State	Zip	Birthday	

Name		Phone	
Address			
City & State	Zip	Birthday	

Name		Phone	
Address			
City & State	Zip	Birthday	

Name		Phone	
Address			
City & State	Zip	Birthday	

Name		Phone	
Address			
City & State	Zip	Birthday	

Name		Phone	
Address			
City & State	Zip	Birthday	

Name		Phone	
Address			
City & State	Zip	Birthday	

Name		Phone	
Address			
City & State	Zip	Birthday	

Name		Phone	
Address			
City & State	Zip	Birthday	

Name		Phone	
Address			
City & State	Zip	Birthday	

Name		Phone	
Address			
City & State	Zip	Birthday	

Name		Phone	
Address			
City & State	Zip	Birthday	

Name		Phone	
Address			
City & State	Zip	Birthday	

JOHN LESLIE BRECK (1860–1899). *Garden at Giverny, c. 1890.*
Oil on canvas, 18 x 21⅞ in. Daniel J. Terra Collection.

Breck was among the earliest colonists at Giverny and one of the first of few to develop strong ties to Monet; he was often invited to paint with the Frenchman and came closer than any of the other foreign artists to being Monet's pupil. This lovely scene of pure color—red and white blooms set amid a multitude of flecked green leaves and stems, with bright yellow pools of sunlight in the foreground—may well have been painted in Monet's garden, as it was the only sizable flower garden in Giverny at the time.

CLAUDE MONET (1840–1926). *Grainstacks, Frost Effect, 1889.*
Oil on canvas, 25½ x 36 in. Hill-Stead Museum, Farmington, Ct.
Fascinated with documenting variations in weather and light, Monet painted several scenes of grain stacks in the fields of Giverny. This one shows the artist's love of frost-filled, snow-covered landscapes and demonstrates his evocative rendering of atmospheric effects: the snow on one side of the grainstacks indicates a bitter, winter wind, and the stronger tones of blue and gray where land and sky meet suggest that the afternoon is rapidly coming to a close. The grain stack paintings illustrate the agrarian life of Monet's Giverny neighbors, whose produce, farm buildings, and houses are depicted in these rural tableaux.

Name Amy Endo (Yasuko)　　yendo@wellesley.edu　Phone 914-368-2994 x1488
Address 25 Shuart Rd.　　　　　　　　　　　beeper: 671-7327
City & State Monsey, NY.　　　　Zip 10952　Birthday 4/12/76

Name　　　　　　　　　　　　　　　　　　　Phone
Address
City & State　　　　　　　　　　Zip　　　　Birthday

Name　　　　　　　　　　　　　　　　　　　Phone
Address
City & State　　　　　　　　　　Zip　　　　Birthday

Name　　　　　　　　　　　　　　　　　　　Phone
Address
City & State　　　　　　　　　　Zip　　　　Birthday

Name　　　　　　　　　　　　　　　　　　　Phone
Address
City & State　　　　　　　　　　Zip　　　　Birthday

Name　　　　　　　　　　　　　　　　　　　Phone
Address
City & State　　　　　　　　　　Zip　　　　Birthday

Name　　　　　	　　　　　　　　　　　　　Phone
Address
City & State　　　　　　　　　　Zip　　　　Birthday

Name　　　　　　　　　　　　　　　　　　　Phone
Address
City & State　　　　　　　　　　Zip　　　　Birthday

Name _____ *Phone* _____
Address _____
City & State _____ *Zip* _____ *Birthday* _____

Name _____ *Phone* _____
Address _____
City & State _____ *Zip* _____ *Birthday* _____

Name _____ *Phone* _____
Address _____
City & State _____ *Zip* _____ *Birthday* _____

Name _____ *Phone* _____
Address _____
City & State _____ *Zip* _____ *Birthday* _____

Name _____ *Phone* _____
Address _____
City & State _____ *Zip* _____ *Birthday* _____

Name _____ *Phone* _____
Address _____
City & State _____ *Zip* _____ *Birthday* _____

Name _____ *Phone* _____
Address _____
City & State _____ *Zip* _____ *Birthday* _____

Name _____ *Phone* _____
Address _____
City & State _____ *Zip* _____ *Birthday* _____

Name: Wendy Fung
Address:
City & State: Zip: Birthday:
temp: 66 Whitehall Dr. Tallmadge, OH. 44278   wwhfung@yahoo.com

Name:
Address:
City & State: Zip: Birthday:

Name:
Address:
City & State: Zip: Birthday:

Name:
Address:
City & State: Zip: Birthday:

Name:
Address:
City & State: Zip: Birthday:

Name:
Address:
City & State: Zip: Birthday:

Name:
Address:
City & State: Zip: Birthday:

Name:
Address:
City & State: Zip: Birthday:

Name			Phone	
Address				
City & State		Zip	Birthday	

Name			Phone	
Address				
City & State		Zip	Birthday	

Name			Phone	
Address				
City & State		Zip	Birthday	

Name			Phone	
Address				
City & State		Zip	Birthday	

Name			Phone	
Address				
City & State		Zip	Birthday	

Name			Phone	
Address				
City & State		Zip	Birthday	

Name			Phone	
Address				
City & State		Zip	Birthday	

Name			Phone	
Address				
City & State		Zip	Birthday	

KARL ANDERSON (1874–1956). *The Idlers, August, 1910.*
Oil on canvas, 49⅜ x 51⅝ in. Valparaiso University Museum of Art, Valparaiso, Indiana; Sloan Collection.

Karl Anderson, brother of the noted American playwright Sherwood Anderson, completed this dazzling outdoor scene while visiting his friend Frederick Frieseke in Giverny in 1909–10. Several elements in Anderson's picture bear a striking resemblance to Frieseke's paintings—beautiful women relaxing in a lush colorful setting; a resplendent, reclining nude; a parasol; the decorative patterns in the flowers, leaves, and the women's clothes; and a strong, flat light that allows the colors to vibrate and glow on the canvas.

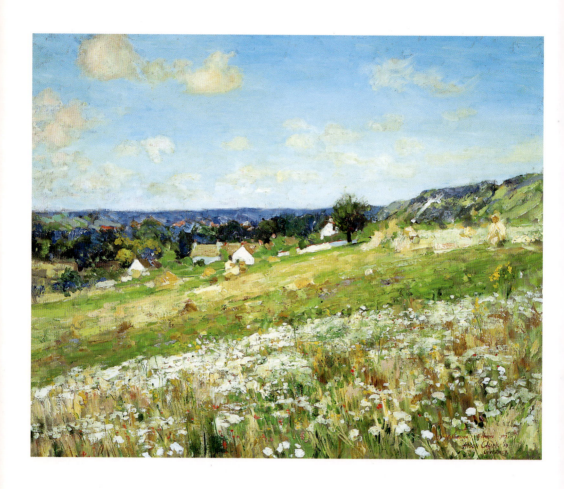

ALSON SKINNER CLARK (1876–1949). *Summer, Giverny, 1910.*
Oil on canvas, 25⅝ x 31⅞ in. Mr. and Mrs. Thomas B. Stiles II.

During his brief stay in Giverny, Chicago native Alson Skinner Clark eschewed images of beautiful women in colorful, enclosed settings for panoramic landscape paintings that resemble Theodore Robinson's canvases from the 1880s. Like Robinson, Clark includes flowering fields, grain stacks, white farm buildings, and blue-green hillsides in his bird's-eye-view of the countryside. Clark's palette is in a higher, brighter key, however, and his short, dot-like strokes of color are more Pointillist than purely Impressionist.

Name Atreyee Gupta   roma@mit.edu   Phone
Address 30 Bellevue Ave.
City & State Winchester, MA.   Zip 01890   Birthday 2/18/77

Name   Phone
Address
City & State   Zip   Birthday

G

Name   Phone
Address
City & State   Zip   Birthday

Name   Phone
Address
City & State   Zip   Birthday

Name   Phone
Address
City & State   Zip   Birthday

Name   Phone
Address
City & State   Zip   Birthday

Name   Phone
Address
City & State   Zip   Birthday

Name   Phone
Address
City & State   Zip   Birthday

Name			Phone	
Address				
City & State		Zip	Birthday	

Name			Phone	
Address				
City & State		Zip	Birthday	

Name			Phone	
Address				
City & State		Zip	Birthday	

Name			Phone	
Address				
City & State		Zip	Birthday	

Name			Phone	
Address				
City & State		Zip	Birthday	

Name			Phone	
Address				
City & State		Zip	Birthday	

Name			Phone	
Address				
City & State		Zip	Birthday	

Name			Phone	
Address				
City & State		Zip	Birthday	

Name _____ *Phone* _____

Address _____

City & State _____ *Zip* _____ *Birthday* _____

Name _____ *Phone* _____

Address _____

City & State _____ *Zip* _____ *Birthday* _____

Name _____ *Phone* _____

Address _____

City & State _____ *Zip* _____ *Birthday* _____

Name _____ *Phone* _____

Address _____

City & State _____ *Zip* _____ *Birthday* _____

Name _____ *Phone* _____

Address _____

City & State _____ *Zip* _____ *Birthday* _____

Name _____ *Phone* _____

Address _____

City & State _____ *Zip* _____ *Birthday* _____

Name _____ *Phone* _____

Address _____

City & State _____ *Zip* _____ *Birthday* _____

Name _____ *Phone* _____

Address _____

City & State _____ *Zip* _____ *Birthday* _____

Name		Phone	
Address			
City & State	Zip	Birthday	

Name		Phone	
Address			
City & State	Zip	Birthday	

Name		Phone	
Address			
City & State	Zip	Birthday	

Name		Phone	
Address			
City & State	Zip	Birthday	

Name		Phone	
Address			
City & State	Zip	Birthday	

Name		Phone	
Address			
City & State	Zip	Birthday	

Name		Phone	
Address			
City & State	Zip	Birthday	

Name		Phone	
Address			
City & State	Zip	Birthday	

LOUIS RITMAN (1889–1963). *Dormitory Breakfast*, 1913.
Oil on canvas, 36 x 36 in. Sheldon Memorial Art Gallery, University of Nebraska–Lincoln; F. M. Hall Collection.

Ritman's style of decorative Impressionism differed from that of his influential colleague Frederick Frieseke in its softer brushstrokes, paler tones, and more clearly delineated compositional elements. In this typical interior study of a woman at a window, there are colorful patterns in the flowers, fabric, and the garden in the background, but the figure and the objects on the table are modeled in light and shade in a more traditional, academic manner. Ritman's pastel color range, soft brushwork, and depiction of rounded female figures recalls the work of French Impressionist Auguste Renoir, who Frieseke also admired.

MARY FAIRCHILD MACMONNIES (1858–1946). *In the Nursery (Giverny Studio), 1897–98.*
Oil on canvas, 32 x 17 in. Daniel J. Terra Collection.

This interior view of the room that served as both MacMonnies' studio and nursery includes the painter's youngest child, Berthe-Hélene, and two women at work, as well as paintings by the celebrated Pierre Puvis de Chavannes, hung on the back wall against one of the MacMonnies' prized tapestries. While the loose brushwork and tones of vibrant white and red indicates the artist's skillful use of Impressionist technique, her subject matter in this work is very different from the rural tableaux of her Giverny predecessors; she has moved the study of color, light, and atmosphere indoors, into the domestic sphere.

Name		Phone	
Address			
City & State	Zip	Birthday	

Name		Phone	
Address			
City & State	Zip	Birthday	

Name		Phone	
Address			
City & State	Zip	Birthday	

Name		Phone	
Address			
City & State	Zip	Birthday	

Name		Phone	
Address			
City & State	Zip	Birthday	

Name		Phone	
Address			
City & State	Zip	Birthday	

Name		Phone	
Address			
City & State	Zip	Birthday	

Name		Phone	
Address			
City & State	Zip	Birthday	

H

Name		Phone	
Address			
City & State	Zip	Birthday	

Name		Phone	
Address			
City & State	Zip	Birthday	

Name		Phone	
Address			
City & State	Zip	Birthday	

Name		Phone	
Address			
City & State	Zip	Birthday	

Name		Phone	
Address			
City & State	Zip	Birthday	

Name		Phone	
Address			
City & State	Zip	Birthday	

Name		Phone	
Address			
City & State	Zip	Birthday	

Name		Phone	
Address			
City & State	Zip	Birthday	

Name _____ *Phone* _____

Address _____

City & State _____ *Zip* _____ *Birthday* _____

Name _____ *Phone* _____

Address _____

City & State _____ *Zip* _____ *Birthday* _____

Name _____ *Phone* _____

Address _____

City & State _____ *Zip* _____ *Birthday* _____

Name _____ *Phone* _____

Address _____

City & State _____ *Zip* _____ *Birthday* _____

Name _____ *Phone* _____

Address _____

City & State _____ *Zip* _____ *Birthday* _____

Name _____ *Phone* _____

Address _____

City & State _____ *Zip* _____ *Birthday* _____

Name _____ *Phone* _____

Address _____

City & State _____ *Zip* _____ *Birthday* _____

Name _____ *Phone* _____

Address _____

City & State _____ *Zip* _____ *Birthday* _____

Name			Phone	
Address				
City & State		Zip	Birthday	

Name			Phone	
Address				
City & State		Zip	Birthday	

Name			Phone	
Address				
City & State		Zip	Birthday	

Name			Phone	
Address				
City & State		Zip	Birthday	

Name			Phone	
Address				
City & State		Zip	Birthday	

Name			Phone	
Address				
City & State		Zip	Birthday	

Name			Phone	
Address				
City & State		Zip	Birthday	

Name			Phone	
Address				
City & State		Zip	Birthday	

WILLIAM BLAIR BRUCE (1859–1906). *The Rainbow, 1888.*
Oil on canvas, 28⅜ x 36¼ in. The Robert McLaughlin Gallery, Oshawa, Canada.

A member of the first generation of Giverny colonists, Canadian William Bruce is credited with the earliest truly Impressionist work done in Giverny by any of the foreign painters. Bruce's paintings from 1887 and 1888—brightly colored, warm-weather landscapes—are characterized by the flecked brushstrokes, sparkling light, and vivid hues that have become synonymous with Impressionism. In this shimmering view of a rainbow appearing after a summer shower, Bruce uses the prismatic subject matter to display the brilliant colorism of his newly adopted aesthetic.

THEODORE BUTLER (1861–1936). The Artist's Family, 1895.
Oil on canvas, 34 x 50 in. Mr. and Mrs. Al Wilsey, San Francisco.

After his marriage to Suzanne Hoschédé, Butler devoted himself to painting scenes of new-found domestic bliss; here, his wife and children enjoy the bright sunlight in the family's Giverny garden. Butler has certainly incorporated the Impressionist techniques of his father-in-law, Monet, into his own art, as the emphasis in this painting is on the study of light and color. Compositional elements, such as the figures and the trees, exist as part of the overall pattern, adding different tones of light and vibrant pastel color to the glowing canvas.

Name		Phone	
Address			
City & State	Zip	Birthday	

Name		Phone	
Address			
City & State	Zip	Birthday	

Name		Phone	
Address			
City & State	Zip	Birthday	

Name		Phone	
Address			
City & State	Zip	Birthday	

Name		Phone	
Address			
City & State	Zip	Birthday	

Name		Phone	
Address			
City & State	Zip	Birthday	

Name		Phone	
Address			
City & State	Zip	Birthday	

Name		Phone	
Address			
City & State	Zip	Birthday	

I J

Name	Phone
Address	
City & State Zip	Birthday

Name	Phone
Address	
City & State Zip	Birthday

Name	Phone
Address	
City & State Zip	Birthday

Name	Phone
Address	
City & State Zip	Birthday

Name	Phone
Address	
City & State Zip	Birthday

Name	Phone
Address	
City & State Zip	Birthday

Name	Phone
Address	
City & State Zip	Birthday

Name	Phone
Address	
City & State Zip	Birthday

Name		Phone	
Address			
City & State	Zip	Birthday	

Name		Phone	
Address			
City & State	Zip	Birthday	

Name		Phone	
Address			
City & State	Zip	Birthday	

Name		Phone	
Address			
City & State	Zip	Birthday	

Name		Phone	
Address			
City & State	Zip	Birthday	

Name		Phone	
Address			
City & State	Zip	Birthday	

Name		Phone	
Address			
City & State	Zip	Birthday	

Name		Phone	
Address			
City & State	Zip	Birthday	

Name _____ *Phone* _____
Address _____
City & State _____ *Zip* _____ *Birthday* _____

Name _____ *Phone* _____
Address _____
City & State _____ *Zip* _____ *Birthday* _____

Name _____ *Phone* _____
Address _____
City & State _____ *Zip* _____ *Birthday* _____

Name _____ *Phone* _____
Address _____
City & State _____ *Zip* _____ *Birthday* _____

Name _____ *Phone* _____
Address _____
City & State _____ *Zip* _____ *Birthday* _____

Name _____ *Phone* _____
Address _____
City & State _____ *Zip* _____ *Birthday* _____

Name _____ *Phone* _____
Address _____
City & State _____ *Zip* _____ *Birthday* _____

Name _____ *Phone* _____
Address _____
City & State _____ *Zip* _____ *Birthday* _____

ELLEN GERTRUDE EMMET RAND (1875–1941). *Madame de Laisemont, 1899.*
Oil on canvas, 17⅜ x 14½ in. Rosina Rand Rossire.

A devoted and talented student of Frederick MacMonnies at the Académie Vitti in Paris, Ellen Emmet rented a house with her sister and her cousin near Giverny during the summer of 1899. All the Emmet women painted, and their letters express tremendous reverence for their mentor. This skillful, penetrating portrait of the Emmets's landlady, executed in quick, loose strokes of white and brown tones, shows MacMonnies' influence in its painterly approach and centered composition; the still life on the table recalls the work of William Merritt Chase, with whom Ellen had previously studied.

MARY HUBBARD FOOTE (1872–1968). *In the Garden, Giverny*, c. 1898–1901.
Oil on canvas, 12½ x 16 in. Private Collection.

A graduate of the Yale School of Fine Arts, Foote came to Paris on a travel grant in 1897, when she became another devoted pupil of Frederick MacMonnies at the Académie Vitti. Foote's admiration of MacMonnies eventually developed into a mutual attraction, however, and they corresponded for years. In Giverny, Foote painted several views of the MacMonnies' celebrated garden, such as this depiction of the colorful border of flowers leading up to a wall in front of the house. Only a portion of the windows and walls are visible; the artist places the viewer at eye-level with the tiny, bright blooms of red, yellow, and white.

Name Pauline Kim (Pastor Paul & Becky JDSN)   pauline-kim@bbns.org   Phone 617-864-5948
Address 254 Concord Ave.
City & State Cambridge, MA.   Zip 02138   Birthday 10/11/80

Name Yoori Kim   Phone
Address
City & State   Zip   Birthday 1/10/80

Name   Phone
Address
City & State   Zip   Birthday

Name   Phone
Address
City & State   Zip   Birthday

Name   Phone
Address
City & State   Zip   Birthday

Name   Phone
Address
City & State   Zip   Birthday

Name   Phone
Address
City & State   Zip   Birthday

Name   Phone
Address
City & State   Zip   Birthday

K

Name			Phone	
Address				
City & State		Zip	Birthday	

Name			Phone	
Address				
City & State		Zip	Birthday	

Name			Phone	
Address				
City & State		Zip	Birthday	

Name			Phone	
Address				
City & State		Zip	Birthday	

Name			Phone	
Address				
City & State		Zip	Birthday	

Name			Phone	
Address				
City & State		Zip	Birthday	

Name			Phone	
Address				
City & State		Zip	Birthday	

Name			Phone	
Address				
City & State		Zip	Birthday	

Name _____ *Phone* _____
Address _____
City & State _____ *Zip* ___ *Birthday* _____

Name _____ *Phone* _____
Address _____
City & State _____ *Zip* ___ *Birthday* _____

Name _____ *Phone* _____
Address _____
City & State _____ *Zip* ___ *Birthday* _____

Name _____ *Phone* _____
Address _____
City & State _____ *Zip* ___ *Birthday* _____

Name _____ *Phone* _____
Address _____
City & State _____ *Zip* ___ *Birthday* _____

Name _____ *Phone* _____
Address _____
City & State _____ *Zip* ___ *Birthday* _____

Name _____ *Phone* _____
Address _____
City & State _____ *Zip* ___ *Birthday* _____

Name _____ *Phone* _____
Address _____
City & State _____ *Zip* ___ *Birthday* _____

Name		Phone
Address		
City & State	Zip	Birthday

Name		Phone
Address		
City & State	Zip	Birthday

Name		Phone
Address		
City & State	Zip	Birthday

Name		Phone
Address		
City & State	Zip	Birthday

Name		Phone
Address		
City & State	Zip	Birthday

Name		Phone
Address		
City & State	Zip	Birthday

Name		Phone
Address		
City & State	Zip	Birthday

Name		Phone
Address		
City & State	Zip	Birthday

HENRY SALEM HUBBELL (1870–1949). By the Fireside, 1909.
Oil on canvas, 74 x 50 in. Central Junior High School, Lawrence, Kansas; Gift of the artist.

Hubbell was perhaps the finest of the many traditional figure painters who came to Giverny during the early years of the twentieth century. Interior views of tranquil, beautifully attired women had become a dominant artistic theme among Hubbell's American colleagues, and this one was especially acclaimed for its distinctive colors. The contrasting pattern in the woman's garment in the foreground, the sprinkling of vivid red on all the fabrics and in the fire, and the glowing umber of one of the sitter's hair, all contained within soft tones of white and gray, reflect the influence of the Impressionist aesthetic.

GUY ROSE (1867–1925). *Untitled (River Epte, Giverny),* c. 1904–12.
Oil on canvas, 23 x 28½ in. James and Linda Ries.

This river view bears a thematic resemblance to one that Rose painted during his first trip to Giverny in 1890, when he was invited by Theodore Butler. The earlier painting, however, is much more naturalistic than this later, more vivid image. Here Rose adopts the tenets of Impressionism by depicting the lush landscape and sparkling water in luminous tones of green, yellow, orange, and blue; the whole scene glows with the warmth of midsummer sunlight.

Name Konny Ly   Phone
Address
City & State   Zip   Birthday 6/15/77

left at stop... pass farm... rt onto mass ave... left farm...

Name Janet Liu   jlui1@wellesley.edu   Phone 862-1494 x1919 + 1st rt.
Address 15 Drew Ave.
City & State Lexington, MA.   Zip 02173   Birthday 10/12/75

Name Yeny Lee   Phone 617-623-5392
Address 783 Broadway St.   beeper: 758-7458
City & State Somerville, MA.   Zip 02144   Birthday 4/29/93

Name Teresa Liu   tlill@mit.edu   Phone 713-488-0212
Address 906 Bridge Hollow Ct.
City & State Houston, TX. 77062   Zip   Birthday 7/12/77   L

Name   Phone
Address
City & State   Zip   Birthday

Name   Phone
Address
City & State   Zip   Birthday

Name   Phone
Address
City & State   Zip   Birthday

Name   Phone
Address
City & State   Zip   Birthday

Name	Phone
Address	
City & State Zip	Birthday

Name	Phone
Address	
City & State Zip	Birthday

Name	Phone
Address	
City & State Zip	Birthday

Name	Phone
Address	
City & State Zip	Birthday

Name	Phone
Address	
City & State Zip	Birthday

Name	Phone
Address	
City & State Zip	Birthday

Name	Phone
Address	
City & State Zip	Birthday

Name	Phone
Address	
City & State Zip	Birthday

Name   *Phone*

Address

City & State   *Zip*   *Birthday*

Name   *Phone*

Address

City & State   *Zip*   *Birthday*

Name   *Phone*

Address

City & State   *Zip*   *Birthday*

Name   *Phone*

Address

City & State   *Zip*   *Birthday*

Name   *Phone*

Address

City & State   *Zip*   *Birthday*

Name   *Phone*

Address

City & State   *Zip*   *Birthday*

Name   *Phone*

Address

City & State   *Zip*   *Birthday*

Name   *Phone*

Address

City & State   *Zip*   *Birthday*

Name		Phone	
Address			
City & State	Zip	Birthday	

Name		Phone	
Address			
City & State	Zip	Birthday	

Name		Phone	
Address			
City & State	Zip	Birthday	

Name		Phone	
Address			
City & State	Zip	Birthday	

Name		Phone	
Address			
City & State	Zip	Birthday	

Name		Phone	
Address			
City & State	Zip	Birthday	

Name		Phone	
Address			
City & State	Zip	Birthday	

Name		Phone	
Address			
City & State	Zip	Birthday	

WILL HICKOK LOW (1853–1932). *The Spinet and the Harp, 1901.*
Oil on canvas, 21¼ x 28¾ in. Dr. and Mrs. Robert W. Lasky, Jr.

This elegant interior view depicting Mary MacMonnies at the harp and (presumably) her daughter Berthe at the spinet was exhibited in New York in 1902. The rich, vibrant colors of the wall covering, rug, and the women's clothing, as well as the detailed craftsmanship of the musical instruments, attest to the luxury and refinement of the MacMonnies household. Low confined most of his subjects and settings to the MacMonnies' compound, in part because of his growing affection for his hostess and future wife (whose own husband was increasingly attracted to his students).

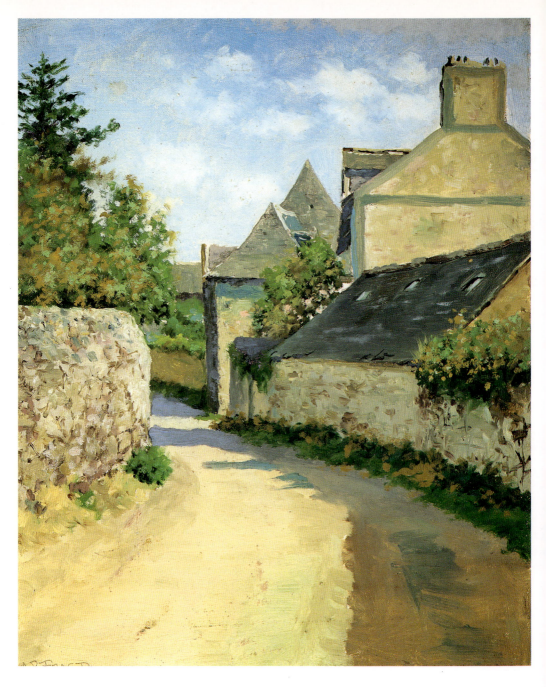

ARTHUR B. FROST (1851–1928). *French Landscape (Giverny Scene)*, c. 1909.
Oil on canvas, 15½ x 12½ in. Virginia and Bernard Demoreuille.

Arthur B. Frost was a highly successful illustrator who came to Giverny in 1908 to concentrate on painting. While Frost, who suffered from color blindness, originally denounced Impressionism, this village scene shows a great sensitivity to the play of light and color on the buildings and trees lining the winding road at Giverny. Not long after finishing this work, Frost recognized the importance of capturing tonal variations in depicting the landscape, and, frustrated by his color blindness, returned to illustration as his principal career.

Name _____ *Phone* _____

Address _____

City & State _____ *Zip* _____ *Birthday* _____

Name _____ *Phone* _____

Address _____

City & State _____ *Zip* _____ *Birthday* _____

Name _____ *Phone* _____

Address _____

City & State _____ *Zip* _____ *Birthday* _____

Name _____ *Phone* _____

Address _____

City & State _____ *Zip* _____ *Birthday* _____

Name _____ *Phone* _____   M

Address _____

City & State _____ *Zip* _____ *Birthday* _____

Name _____ *Phone* _____

Address _____

City & State _____ *Zip* _____ *Birthday* _____

Name _____ *Phone* _____

Address _____

City & State _____ *Zip* _____ *Birthday* _____

Name _____ *Phone* _____

Address _____

City & State _____ *Zip* _____ *Birthday* _____

Name	Phone
Address	
City & State Zip	Birthday
Name	Phone
Address	
City & State Zip	Birthday
Name	Phone
Address	
City & State Zip	Birthday
Name	Phone
Address	
City & State Zip	Birthday
Name	Phone
Address	
City & State Zip	Birthday
Name	Phone
Address	
City & State Zip	Birthday
Name	Phone
Address	
City & State Zip	Birthday
Name	Phone
Address	
City & State Zip	Birthday

Name _____ *Phone* _____

Address _____

City & State _____ *Zip* ___ *Birthday* _____

Name _____ *Phone* _____

Address _____

City & State _____ *Zip* ___ *Birthday* _____

Name _____ *Phone* _____

Address _____

City & State _____ *Zip* ___ *Birthday* _____

Name _____ *Phone* _____

Address _____

City & State _____ *Zip* ___ *Birthday* _____

Name _____ *Phone* _____

Address _____

City & State _____ *Zip* ___ *Birthday* _____

Name _____ *Phone* _____

Address _____

City & State _____ *Zip* ___ *Birthday* _____

Name _____ *Phone* _____

Address _____

City & State _____ *Zip* ___ *Birthday* _____

Name _____ *Phone* _____

Address _____

City & State _____ *Zip* ___ *Birthday* _____

Name		*Phone*	
Address			
City & State	*Zip*	*Birthday*	

Name _____ *Phone* _____
Address _____
City & State _____ *Zip* _____ *Birthday* _____

Name _____ *Phone* _____
Address _____
City & State _____ *Zip* _____ *Birthday* _____

Name _____ *Phone* _____
Address _____
City & State _____ *Zip* _____ *Birthday* _____

Name _____ *Phone* _____
Address _____
City & State _____ *Zip* _____ *Birthday* _____

Name _____ *Phone* _____
Address _____
City & State _____ *Zip* _____ *Birthday* _____

Name _____ *Phone* _____
Address _____
City & State _____ *Zip* _____ *Birthday* _____

Name _____ *Phone* _____
Address _____
City & State _____ *Zip* _____ *Birthday* _____

Name _____ *Phone* _____
Address _____
City & State _____ *Zip* _____ *Birthday* _____

MARY FAIRCHILD MACMONNIES (1858–1946). *Roses and Lilies, 1897.*
Oil on canvas, 52⅛ x 69½ in. Musée des Beaux-Arts de Rouen, Rouen, France.

Mary MacMonnies and her husband, the sculptor Frederick MacMonnies, settled in Giverny in 1893 and became the presiding influence over the second generation of colonists. An accomplished Impressionist painter, Mary MacMonnies employed her mastery of free brushwork and vivid color in paintings of her family members, house, and gardens. This colorful, sun-drenched portrait of the artist with her youngest child won a gold medal at the Exposition Universelle in Paris in 1900.

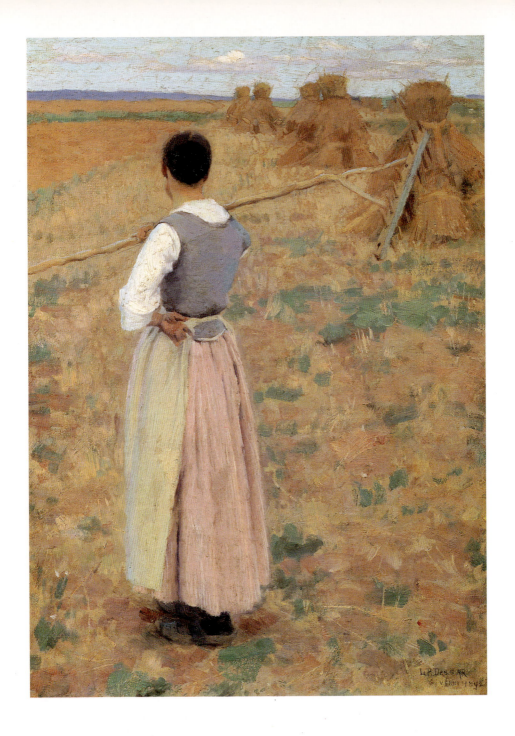

LOUIS PAUL DESSAR (1867–1952). *Peasant Woman and Haystacks, Giverny, 1892.*
Oil on canvas, 18¼ x 13 in. Terra Foundation for the Arts; Daniel J. Terra Collection.

The tradition of depicting peasants at work in the landscape that was begun by Jean-François Millet and the Barbizon school painters was continued in Giverny by many of the colonists. American painter Louis Paul Dessar created this archetypal peasant image: a lone female figure in peasant garb, her back turned toward the viewer, looking out toward a line of grain stacks that lead into a seemingly endless field.

Name Amy Ng   awn@mit.edu   Phone 713-265-4006
Address 3306 Sturbridge Ln.
City & State Sugar Land, TX. 77479   Zip   Birthday 7/4/77

Name   Phone
Address
City & State   Zip   Birthday

Name   Phone
Address
City & State   Zip   Birthday

Name   Phone
Address
City & State   Zip   Birthday

Name   Phone
Address
City & State   Zip   Birthday

Name   Phone
Address
City & State   Zip   Birthday

Name   Phone
Address
City & State   Zip   Birthday

Name   Phone
Address
City & State   Zip   Birthday

Name		Phone	
Address			
City & State	Zip	Birthday	

Name		Phone	
Address			
City & State	Zip	Birthday	

Name		Phone	
Address			
City & State	Zip	Birthday	

Name		Phone	
Address			
City & State	Zip	Birthday	

Name		Phone	
Address			
City & State	Zip	Birthday	

Name		Phone	
Address			
City & State	Zip	Birthday	

Name		Phone	
Address			
City & State	Zip	Birthday	

Name		Phone	
Address			
City & State	Zip	Birthday	

Name		*Phone*
Address		
City & State	*Zip*	*Birthday*

Name		*Phone*
Address		
City & State	*Zip*	*Birthday*

Name		*Phone*
Address		
City & State	*Zip*	*Birthday*

Name		*Phone*
Address		
City & State	*Zip*	*Birthday*

Name		*Phone*
Address		
City & State	*Zip*	*Birthday*

Name		*Phone*
Address		
City & State	*Zip*	*Birthday*

Name		*Phone*
Address		
City & State	*Zip*	*Birthday*

Name		*Phone*
Address		
City & State	*Zip*	*Birthday*

Name			Phone	
Address				
City & State		Zip	Birthday	

Name			Phone	
Address				
City & State		Zip	Birthday	

Name			Phone	
Address				
City & State		Zip	Birthday	

Name			Phone	
Address				
City & State		Zip	Birthday	

Name			Phone	
Address				
City & State		Zip	Birthday	

Name			Phone	
Address				
City & State		Zip	Birthday	

Name			Phone	
Address				
City & State		Zip	Birthday	

Name			Phone	
Address				
City & State		Zip	Birthday	

LOUIS RITTER (1854–1892). *Willows and Stream, Giverny, 1887.*
Oil on canvas, 25⅞ x 21⅜ in. Terra Foundation for the Arts; Daniel J. Terra Collection.

Ritter was among the handful of painters who founded the American artists' colony at Giverny in 1887. Ritter and his companions were in search of a summer home when they happened upon the little village on the Epte river; Monet's presence had not directly drawn them there. Ritter's streamside scene is closer to Barbizon naturalism than to Monet's Impressionism; the branches, stones, and reflections of the trees are accurately delineated, and his palette is more somber than the sun-splashed hues seen in Monet's work.

WILLIAM DE LEFTWICH DODGE (1876–1935). *In MacMonnies' Giverny Garden,* c. 1898–99. Oil on canvas, 50 x 33½ in. Mr. and Mrs. Martin Kodner, Saint Louis; Courtesy of Gallery of the Masters, Inc., Saint Louis.

An academically trained artist, Dodge created his most ambitious works in Mary and Frederick MacMonnies' garden, such as this view of a woman looking into a reflecting pool where her white gown and the warm tones of the summer foliage are exquisitely reproduced with loose, Impressionist brushstrokes. Enveloped in a golden glow, the painting projects an eternal, almost mythical image even as it captures a fleeting moment. Dodge is also credited with popularizing the theme of the nude in the garden, as he often painted his model, Georgette, reclining naked amid the flowers and trees of Giverny.

Name			Phone	
Address				
City & State		Zip	Birthday	

Name			Phone	
Address				
City & State		Zip	Birthday	

Name			Phone	
Address				
City & State		Zip	Birthday	

Name			Phone	
Address				
City & State		Zip	Birthday	

Name			Phone	
Address				
City & State		Zip	Birthday	

O

Name			Phone	
Address				
City & State		Zip	Birthday	

Name			Phone	
Address				
City & State		Zip	Birthday	

Name			Phone	
Address				
City & State		Zip	Birthday	

Name			Phone	
Address				
City & State		Zip	Birthday	

Name			Phone	
Address				
City & State		Zip	Birthday	

Name			Phone	
Address				
City & State		Zip	Birthday	

Name			Phone	
Address				
City & State		Zip	Birthday	

Name			Phone	
Address				
City & State		Zip	Birthday	

Name			Phone	
Address				
City & State		Zip	Birthday	

Name			Phone	
Address				
City & State		Zip	Birthday	

Name			Phone	
Address				
City & State		Zip	Birthday	

Name _____ *Phone* _____
Address _____
City & State _____ *Zip* ___ *Birthday* _____

Name _____ *Phone* _____
Address _____
City & State _____ *Zip* ___ *Birthday* _____

Name _____ *Phone* _____
Address _____
City & State _____ *Zip* ___ *Birthday* _____

Name _____ *Phone* _____
Address _____
City & State _____ *Zip* ___ *Birthday* _____

Name _____ *Phone* _____
Address _____
City & State _____ *Zip* ___ *Birthday* _____

Name _____ *Phone* _____
Address _____
City & State _____ *Zip* ___ *Birthday* _____

Name _____ *Phone* _____
Address _____
City & State _____ *Zip* ___ *Birthday* _____

Name _____ *Phone* _____
Address _____
City & State _____ *Zip* ___ *Birthday* _____

Name _____ *Phone* _____

Address _____

City & State _____ *Zip* _____ *Birthday* _____

Name _____ *Phone* _____

Address _____

City & State _____ *Zip* _____ *Birthday* _____

Name _____ *Phone* _____

Address _____

City & State _____ *Zip* _____ *Birthday* _____

Name _____ *Phone* _____

Address _____

City & State _____ *Zip* _____ *Birthday* _____

Name _____ *Phone* _____

Address _____

City & State _____ *Zip* _____ *Birthday* _____

Name _____ *Phone* _____

Address _____

City & State _____ *Zip* _____ *Birthday* _____

Name _____ *Phone* _____

Address _____

City & State _____ *Zip* _____ *Birthday* _____

Name _____ *Phone* _____

Address _____

City & State _____ *Zip* _____ *Birthday* _____

GEORGE ALBERT THOMPSON (1868–1938). *A View of Giverny, France, 1897.*
Oil on canvas, 21⅜ x 25¾ in. Private collection; Courtesy of Spanierman Gallery, New York.

Thompson was a graduate of the Yale School of the Fine Arts who came to Giverny in 1896 as part of the second generation of colonists. This blue, green, and gold landscape, which actually depicts not Giverny but nearby Vernon, incorporates the brilliant color of Monet's canvases with the panoramic perspective that his American predecessors Theodore Robinson and John Leslie Breck employed in earlier views of Giverny. The painting is both a study of color and light in a lush landscape and a detailed rendering of its elements—fields, trees, village buildings, and rising hillsides.

THEODORE ROBINSON (1852–1896). *The Wedding March*, 1892.
Oil on canvas, 22⅝ x 26½ in. Daniel J. Terra Collection.

A close friend of Monet's, Robinson commemorated the marriage of Monet's stepdaughter, Suzanne Hoschedé, to the American painter Theodore Butler with this sparkling, sun-drenched view of the family on their way to the wedding ceremony. The painting is not only a masterpiece of Impressionism, but a visual record of a significant event in the life of the colony. Swathed in a filmy white veil, Suzanne walks with Monet, followed by her mother and Butler, all bathed in sunlight.

Name: Tammy Provencio
Address: 783 Broadway St.
City & State: Somerville, MA.   Zip: 02144
Phone: 617-623-5392/258-5521
cell: 872-2304
beeper: 458-6708 tammyp@mit.edu
Birthday: 7/18/68

Name: Chris/Sally SMN (Pak) [JDSN above Chris]
Address: 12 Goldstar Rd.
City & State: Cambridge, MA.   Zip: 02140
Phone: 876-8594 (h)
Birthday: 5/23/64, 5/5/66

P

Name			Phone	
Address				
City & State		Zip	Birthday	

Name			Phone	
Address				
City & State		Zip	Birthday	

Name			Phone	
Address				
City & State		Zip	Birthday	

Name			Phone	
Address				
City & State		Zip	Birthday	

Name			Phone	
Address				
City & State		Zip	Birthday	

Name			Phone	
Address				
City & State		Zip	Birthday	

Name			Phone	
Address				
City & State		Zip	Birthday	

Name			Phone	
Address				
City & State		Zip	Birthday	

Name _____ *Phone* _____
Address _____
City & State _____ *Zip* _____ *Birthday* _____

Name _____ *Phone* _____
Address _____
City & State _____ *Zip* _____ *Birthday* _____

Name _____ *Phone* _____
Address _____
City & State _____ *Zip* _____ *Birthday* _____

Name _____ *Phone* _____
Address _____
City & State _____ *Zip* _____ *Birthday* _____

Name _____ *Phone* _____
Address _____
City & State _____ *Zip* _____ *Birthday* _____

Name _____ *Phone* _____
Address _____
City & State _____ *Zip* _____ *Birthday* _____

Name _____ *Phone* _____
Address _____
City & State _____ *Zip* _____ *Birthday* _____

Name _____ *Phone* _____
Address _____
City & State _____ *Zip* _____ *Birthday* _____

Name		Phone	
Address			
City & State	Zip	Birthday	

Name		Phone	
Address			
City & State	Zip	Birthday	

Name		Phone	
Address			
City & State	Zip	Birthday	

Name		Phone	
Address			
City & State	Zip	Birthday	

Name		Phone	
Address			
City & State	Zip	Birthday	

Name		Phone	
Address			
City & State	Zip	Birthday	

Name		Phone	
Address			
City & State	Zip	Birthday	

Name		Phone	
Address			
City & State	Zip	Birthday	

FREDERICK FRIESEKE (1874–1939). *Misty Morn, c. 1908–09.*
Oil on canvas, 26 x 32¼ in. Max N. and Heidi L. Berry.

Frieseke's paintings of traditional landscape themes, such as this view of the willow-bordered Epte river, are less experimental than his figural works. The loose brushwork, dappled light and shadow, and soft haze enveloping this early-morning scene are Impressionist strategies employed by the Giverny painters both of his day and of earlier decades. Like his predecessor and friend Theodore Robinson, Frieseke was often specific in his portrayal of the Giverny countryside, painting recognizable views of the river, the fields, and the town.

LOUIS RITMAN (1889–1963). *Early Morning Sunshine, 1912–14.*
Oil on canvas, 36 x 29 ¼ in. Private collection, Pennsylvania; Courtesy of Spanierman Gallery, New York.

The last of the many midwesterners who formed the Giverny group, Louis Ritman applied the methods of decorative Impressionism to various interior subjects. This boudoir scene of a partially clothed woman at the window allowed the artist to create a contrast between a shaded interior and brilliant sunlight. The whole canvas is filled with lively, colorful patterns, from the fruit, china, and bedcovering to the woman's gown, the curtain, and the sparkling garden, whose flowers and foliage blend into the same plane as the drapery, one window pane, and the outline of the woman's body.

Name		Phone	
Address			
City & State	Zip	Birthday	

Name		Phone	
Address			
City & State	Zip	Birthday	

Name		Phone	
Address			
City & State	Zip	Birthday	

Name		Phone	
Address			
City & State	Zip	Birthday	

Name		Phone	
Address			
City & State	Zip	Birthday	

Name		Phone	
Address			
City & State	Zip	Birthday	

Name		Phone	
Address			
City & State	Zip	Birthday	

Q R

Name		Phone	
Address			
City & State	Zip	Birthday	

Name			Phone	
Address				
City & State		Zip	Birthday	

Name			Phone	
Address				
City & State		Zip	Birthday	

Name			Phone	
Address				
City & State		Zip	Birthday	

Name			Phone	
Address				
City & State		Zip	Birthday	

Name			Phone	
Address				
City & State		Zip	Birthday	

Name			Phone	
Address				
City & State		Zip	Birthday	

Name			Phone	
Address				
City & State		Zip	Birthday	

Name			Phone	
Address				
City & State		Zip	Birthday	

Name	*Phone*
Address	
City & State *Zip*	*Birthday*

Name	*Phone*
Address	
City & State *Zip*	*Birthday*

Name	*Phone*
Address	
City & State *Zip*	*Birthday*

Name	*Phone*
Address	
City & State *Zip*	*Birthday*

Name	*Phone*
Address	
City & State *Zip*	*Birthday*

Name	*Phone*
Address	
City & State *Zip*	*Birthday*

Name	*Phone*
Address	
City & State *Zip*	*Birthday*

Name	*Phone*
Address	
City & State *Zip*	*Birthday*

Name			Phone	
Address				
City & State		Zip	Birthday	

Name			Phone	
Address				
City & State		Zip	Birthday	

Name			Phone	
Address				
City & State		Zip	Birthday	

Name			Phone	
Address				
City & State		Zip	Birthday	

Name			Phone	
Address				
City & State		Zip	Birthday	

Name			Phone	
Address				
City & State		Zip	Birthday	

Name			Phone	
Address				
City & State		Zip	Birthday	

Name			Phone	
Address				
City & State		Zip	Birthday	

FREDERICK MACMONNIES (1863–1937). *Mrs.MacMonnies, Betty and Marjorie, 1901.*
Oil on canvas, 96½ x 88½ in. Musée des Beaux-Arts de Rouen, Rouen, France.

MacMonnies was already widely renowned as a sculptor when his family moved to Giverny in 1893, but during the next decade he began to pursue a career in painting alongside his wife, Mary. Portraits, figure studies, and family scenes were his favorite subject matter, and his style was more academic than his wife's. The setting for this monumental family portrait is decidedly Impressionist—a garden bathed in full, brilliant sunlight—but each dark green leaf is individually drawn, and the solid forms of the figures and the trees are carefully modeled.

GUY ROSE (1867–1925). *The Blue Kimono*, c.1909.
Oil on canvas, 31 x 19 in. Terry and Paul Trotter; Trotter Galleries.

Like many other members of the third generation of Giverny colonists (who arrived during the early 1900s), California native Guy Rose completed a number of figure paintings while working there. The ideal subject matter for these popular figure studies is illustrated in Rose's striking image of a woman wearing a brilliant blue gown: a young female model posed in a secluded garden bursting with color and bathed in sunlight. Rose's identification of the dress as a kimono is indicative of the influence that Japanese art and culture had on many Impressionist painters.

Name: Julie Shin joolzvrn@mit.edu Phone: 310-377-4796
Address: P.O. Box 3062
City & State: Palos Verdes Peninsula, CA. Zip: 90274 Birthday: 2/1/77

Name **Sarah Shepard**
Address **11 Hill St. P.O. Box 79** ~~Woodvi~~
City & State **Woodville, MA. 01784**   Zip
Phone **508-435-5116 x71?**
sshepard@fia.net / sshepard (wellesley)
Birthday **11/12/78**

Name **Missy Samiagio**
Address
City & State   Zip
Cape: 508-477-1354
Phone
Birthday

Name
Address
City & State   Zip
Phone
Birthday

Name
Address
City & State   Zip
Phone
Birthday

Name
Address
City & State   Zip
Phone
Birthday

Name
Address
City & State   Zip
Phone
Birthday

Name
Address
City & State   Zip
Phone
Birthday

Name
Address
City & State   Zip
Phone
Birthday

Name _____ *Phone* _____

Address _____

City & State _____ *Zip* _____ *Birthday* _____

Name _____ *Phone* _____

Address _____

City & State _____ *Zip* _____ *Birthday* _____

Name _____ *Phone* _____

Address _____

City & State _____ *Zip* _____ *Birthday* _____

Name _____ *Phone* _____

Address _____

City & State _____ *Zip* _____ *Birthday* _____

Name _____ *Phone* _____

Address _____

City & State _____ *Zip* _____ *Birthday* _____

Name _____ *Phone* _____

Address _____

City & State _____ *Zip* _____ *Birthday* _____

Name _____ *Phone* _____

Address _____

City & State _____ *Zip* _____ *Birthday* _____

Name _____ *Phone* _____

Address _____

City & State _____ *Zip* _____ *Birthday* _____

Name _____ *Phone* _____
Address _____
City & State _____ *Zip* _____ *Birthday* _____

Name _____ *Phone* _____
Address _____
City & State _____ *Zip* _____ *Birthday* _____

Name _____ *Phone* _____
Address _____
City & State _____ *Zip* _____ *Birthday* _____

Name _____ *Phone* _____
Address _____
City & State _____ *Zip* _____ *Birthday* _____

Name _____ *Phone* _____
Address _____
City & State _____ *Zip* _____ *Birthday* _____

Name _____ *Phone* _____
Address _____
City & State _____ *Zip* _____ *Birthday* _____

Name _____ *Phone* _____
Address _____
City & State _____ *Zip* _____ *Birthday* _____

Name _____ *Phone* _____
Address _____
City & State _____ *Zip* _____ *Birthday* _____

FREDERICK FRIESEKE (1874–1939). *Lady with a Parasol, c. 1908.*
Oil on canvas, 25½ x 32 in. Cornelia and Meredith Long.

In this painting of his wife, Sadie, Frieseke saturates the whole canvas with intense green; even the woman's sun-splashed gown, patterned jacket, and pale flesh are overcast with a green hue. The stillness of the water also indicates that Frieseke is experimenting with non-Impressionist strategies. There are no oars, no waves, no movement visible here; the artist has not captured a fleeting moment, but an unchanging, almost imaginary scene—a work of art, not of nature.

JOHN LESLIE BRECK (1860–1899). *M. Baudy Behind His Desk at the Café of the Hotel Baudy*, 1888.
Oil on canvas, 13⅜ x 17¼ in. Location unknown.

The Hotel Baudy was the center of all social life for the artists who came to Giverny in the 1880s and 1890s. Lucien Baudy (who is pictured in Breck's painting) and his wife provided food, lodging, and studio space to many of the colonists; almost all of them spent a significant amount of time at the hotel. Within a few years of the first colonists' arrival, the wall and doors of the hotel were covered with the artists' works, which the proprietors often had to accept in lieu of payment.

Name _____ *Phone* _____

Address _____

City & State _____ *Zip* _____ *Birthday* _____

Name _____ *Phone* _____

Address _____

City & State _____ *Zip* _____ *Birthday* _____

Name _____ *Phone* _____

Address _____

City & State _____ *Zip* _____ *Birthday* _____

Name _____ *Phone* _____

Address _____

City & State _____ *Zip* _____ *Birthday* _____

Name _____ *Phone* _____

Address _____

City & State _____ *Zip* _____ *Birthday* _____

Name _____ *Phone* _____

Address _____

City & State _____ *Zip* _____ *Birthday* _____

Name _____ *Phone* _____

Address _____

City & State _____ *Zip* _____ *Birthday* _____

T

Name _____ *Phone* _____

Address _____

City & State _____ *Zip* _____ *Birthday* _____

Name _____ *Phone* _____
Address _____
City & State _____ *Zip* _____ *Birthday* _____

Name _____ *Phone* _____
Address _____
City & State _____ *Zip* _____ *Birthday* _____

Name _____ *Phone* _____
Address _____
City & State _____ *Zip* _____ *Birthday* _____

Name _____ *Phone* _____
Address _____
City & State _____ *Zip* _____ *Birthday* _____

Name _____ *Phone* _____
Address _____
City & State _____ *Zip* _____ *Birthday* _____

Name _____ *Phone* _____
Address _____
City & State _____ *Zip* _____ *Birthday* _____

Name _____ *Phone* _____
Address _____
City & State _____ *Zip* _____ *Birthday* _____

Name _____ *Phone* _____
Address _____
City & State _____ *Zip* _____ *Birthday* _____

Name _____ *Phone* _____
Address _____
City & State _____ *Zip* _____ *Birthday* _____

Name _____ *Phone* _____
Address _____
City & State _____ *Zip* _____ *Birthday* _____

Name _____ *Phone* _____
Address _____
City & State _____ *Zip* _____ *Birthday* _____

Name _____ *Phone* _____
Address _____
City & State _____ *Zip* _____ *Birthday* _____

Name _____ *Phone* _____
Address _____
City & State _____ *Zip* _____ *Birthday* _____

Name _____ *Phone* _____
Address _____
City & State _____ *Zip* _____ *Birthday* _____

Name _____ *Phone* _____
Address _____
City & State _____ *Zip* _____ *Birthday* _____

Name _____ *Phone* _____
Address _____
City & State _____ *Zip* _____ *Birthday* _____

Name		*Phone*
Address		
City & State	*Zip*	*Birthday*

Name		*Phone*
Address		
City & State	*Zip*	*Birthday*

Name		*Phone*
Address		
City & State	*Zip*	*Birthday*

Name		*Phone*
Address		
City & State	*Zip*	*Birthday*

Name		*Phone*
Address		
City & State	*Zip*	*Birthday*

Name		*Phone*
Address		
City & State	*Zip*	*Birthday*

Name		*Phone*
Address		
City & State	*Zip*	*Birthday*

Name		*Phone*
Address		
City & State	*Zip*	*Birthday*

FREDERICK FRIESEKE (1874–1939). *Open Window*, c. 1900.
Oil on canvas, 51½ x 40 in. Randolph and Judith A. Agley Art Collection.

Beautiful women portrayed as art objects are prevalent in Frieseke's work. This one presents the Victorian ideal of womanhoood as a state of confined, domestic bliss, a condition symbolized in the painting by the caged birds. The blazing sunlight illuminates the blending and contrasting patterns in the yellow and green flowers, the woman's striped dress, the golden cage, and even the shadow on the window. Frieseke's innovative use of unnatural light and interlocking patterns allies his work to that of Post-Impressionists Pierre Bonnard and Edouard Vuillard.

PHILIP LESLIE HALE (1865–1931). *French Farmhouse, 1890–94.*
Oil on canvas, 25½ x 31⅞ in. Museum of Fine Arts, Boston; Gift of Nancy Hale Bowers.

In 1888, Hale arrived in Giverny an academic naturalist painter, but the influence of his idyllic, sunlit surroundings—and, most likely, of his colleagues' experimentation—transformed his work. Before long he adopted the bright palette of the Impressionists and began using the small Pointillist brushstrokes developed by the Neo-Impressionists Georges Seurat and Paul Signac. *French Farmhouse*, with its limited, pastel tonal range and tiny, shimmering daubs of paint, illustrates Hale's unique application of the Pointillist method to a Giverny subject.

Name	*Phone*
Address	
City & State *Zip*	*Birthday*
Name	*Phone*
Address	
City & State *Zip*	*Birthday*
Name	*Phone*
Address	
City & State *Zip*	*Birthday*
Name	*Phone*
Address	
City & State *Zip*	*Birthday*
Name	*Phone*
Address	
City & State *Zip*	*Birthday*
Name	*Phone*
Address	
City & State *Zip*	*Birthday*
Name	*Phone*
Address	
City & State *Zip*	*Birthday*
Name	*Phone*
Address	
City & State *Zip*	*Birthday*

U
V

Name		*Phone*	
Address			
City & State	*Zip*	*Birthday*	

Name _____ *Phone* _____
Address _____
City & State _____ *Zip* _____ *Birthday* _____

Name _____ *Phone* _____
Address _____
City & State _____ *Zip* _____ *Birthday* _____

Name _____ *Phone* _____
Address _____
City & State _____ *Zip* _____ *Birthday* _____

Name _____ *Phone* _____
Address _____
City & State _____ *Zip* _____ *Birthday* _____

Name _____ *Phone* _____
Address _____
City & State _____ *Zip* _____ *Birthday* _____

Name _____ *Phone* _____
Address _____
City & State _____ *Zip* _____ *Birthday* _____

Name _____ *Phone* _____
Address _____
City & State _____ *Zip* _____ *Birthday* _____

Name _____ *Phone* _____
Address _____
City & State _____ *Zip* _____ *Birthday* _____

Name _____ *Phone* _____

Address _____

City & State _____ *Zip* _____ *Birthday* _____

Name _____ *Phone* _____

Address _____

City & State _____ *Zip* _____ *Birthday* _____

Name _____ *Phone* _____

Address _____

City & State _____ *Zip* _____ *Birthday* _____

Name _____ *Phone* _____

Address _____

City & State _____ *Zip* _____ *Birthday* _____

Name _____ *Phone* _____

Address _____

City & State _____ *Zip* _____ *Birthday* _____

Name _____ *Phone* _____

Address _____

City & State _____ *Zip* _____ *Birthday* _____

Name _____ *Phone* _____

Address _____

City & State _____ *Zip* _____ *Birthday* _____

Name _____ *Phone* _____

Address _____

City & State _____ *Zip* _____ *Birthday* _____

Name		Phone	
Address			
City & State	Zip	Birthday	

Name		Phone	
Address			
City & State	Zip	Birthday	

Name		Phone	
Address			
City & State	Zip	Birthday	

Name		Phone	
Address			
City & State	Zip	Birthday	

Name		Phone	
Address			
City & State	Zip	Birthday	

Name		Phone	
Address			
City & State	Zip	Birthday	

Name		Phone	
Address			
City & State	Zip	Birthday	

Name		Phone	
Address			
City & State	Zip	Birthday	

WILL HICKOK LOW (1853–1932). *Interlude: MacMonnies' Garden, 1901.*
Oil on canvas, 19 1/4 x 25 1/4 in. Bayly Art Museum of the University of Virginia, Charlottesville.

A well-known muralist when he came to paint in Giverny with the MacMonnies, Low eventually married Mary MacMonnies in 1909 after her divorce from Frederick. Here, Low interprets the MacMonnies' prized garden in classical terms, transforming it into a fanciful setting for two women, one with a harp, both clad in ancient garb. While Low has staged his painting in the past, his attention to atmospheric effects— the soft, afternoon sunlight crossing the garden wall, surrounding the women, and reflected in the pool— demonstrates his awareness of the Impressionist emphasis on temporal variations in light and color.

MARY HUBBARD FOOTE (1872–1968). *View Through the Studio Window, Giverny*, c. 1899–1901. Oil on canvas, 25 1/2 x 18 in. Courtesy of John Pence Gallery, San Francisco.

Foote applies a unique approach to a typical Giverny subject by framing this view of an enclosed garden with a window opening toward the viewer. From the darker, shadowy space in front of the sunlit sill and white-curtained window, we are invited out into the colorful garden and beckoned past the gate into the tree-lined hills. Mary Foote enjoyed a promising early career and entered into a romantic relationship with her teacher, Frederick MacMonnies. She left France in 1901, however, and after a nervous breakdown in 1920 she gave up painting and became a disciple of Carl Jung in Zurich.

Name Sophia Wang swang@wellesley.edu Phone 718-786-3055 x7609
Address 39-59 47th St.
City & State Sunnyside, NY. Zip 11104 Birthday 5/17/1976

Name Phone
Address
City & State Zip Birthday

Name Phone
Address
City & State Zip Birthday

Name Phone
Address
City & State Zip Birthday

Name Phone
Address
City & State Zip Birthday

Name Phone
Address
City & State Zip Birthday

Name Phone
Address
City & State Zip Birthday

Name Phone
Address
City & State Zip Birthday

W

Name		Phone	
Address			
City & State	Zip	Birthday	

Name		Phone	
Address			
City & State	Zip	Birthday	

Name		Phone	
Address			
City & State	Zip	Birthday	

Name		Phone	
Address			
City & State	Zip	Birthday	

Name		Phone	
Address			
City & State	Zip	Birthday	

Name		Phone	
Address			
City & State	Zip	Birthday	

Name		Phone	
Address			
City & State	Zip	Birthday	

Name		Phone	
Address			
City & State	Zip	Birthday	

Name _____ *Phone* _____

Address _____

City & State _____ *Zip* _____ *Birthday* _____

Name _____ *Phone* _____

Address _____

City & State _____ *Zip* _____ *Birthday* _____

Name _____ *Phone* _____

Address _____

City & State _____ *Zip* _____ *Birthday* _____

Name _____ *Phone* _____

Address _____

City & State _____ *Zip* _____ *Birthday* _____

Name _____ *Phone* _____

Address _____

City & State _____ *Zip* _____ *Birthday* _____

Name _____ *Phone* _____

Address _____

City & State _____ *Zip* _____ *Birthday* _____

Name _____ *Phone* _____

Address _____

City & State _____ *Zip* _____ *Birthday* _____

Name _____ *Phone* _____

Address _____

City & State _____ *Zip* _____ *Birthday* _____

Name			Phone	
Address				
City & State		Zip	Birthday	

Name			Phone	
Address				
City & State		Zip	Birthday	

Name			Phone	
Address				
City & State		Zip	Birthday	

Name			Phone	
Address				
City & State		Zip	Birthday	

Name			Phone	
Address				
City & State		Zip	Birthday	

Name			Phone	
Address				
City & State		Zip	Birthday	

Name			Phone	
Address				
City & State		Zip	Birthday	

Name			Phone	
Address				
City & State		Zip	Birthday	

PIERRE BONNARD (1867–1947). *Dining Room in the Country*, 1913.
Oil on canvas, 64 3/4 x 81 in. The Minneapolis Institute of Arts.

Throughout the life of the colony, Monet was the only French painter who lived in Giverny; the town was dominated by American artists. The Nabi painter Pierre Bonnard lived downriver in nearby Veronnet, isolated from the Americans. Bonnard however, like Frieseke, was investigating the use of a decorative pictorial plane and a bright, variegated palette. In this striking interior, the flat colors on the door, walls, and furniture contrast sharply with the vibrant patterns in the garden; yet the woman leaning on the sill blends into her surroundings, creating the illusion of a two-dimensional image—a painting within the painting.

LAWTON S. PARKER (1868–1954). *Woman in a Boat,* c. 1910.
Oil on canvas, 30 x 24 in. David Ramus Fine Art, New York and Atlanta.

Lawton, who arrived in Giverny in 1903, was the artist most influenced by Frederick Frieseke, and he adapted many of Frieseke's themes and innovations. Parker's version of the woman-in-a-boat motif so common in the work of the Giverny painters is a sunlit study in pastels. As in Frieseke's paintings, Parker uses different hues to blend, complement, and contrast harmoniously, although Parker's tones are softer than Frieseke's and there is no decorative patterning. The image itself is slightly melancholy; the woman's head is downcast, her face covered in shadow.

Name Judy Yeh   jyeh@wellesley.edu   Phone 718-526-2375 x7499
Address 150-15 87th Ave.
City & State Jamaica, NY.   Zip 11432   Birthday 5/3/78

Name Sara Yoon   Phone
Address
City & State Dallas, TX.   Zip   Birthday

Name   Phone
Address
City & State   Zip   Birthday

Name   Phone
Address
City & State   Zip   Birthday

Name   Phone
Address
City & State   Zip   Birthday

Name   Phone
Address
City & State   Zip   Birthday

Name   Phone
Address
City & State   Zip   Birthday

Name   Phone
Address
City & State   Zip   Birthday

X Y Z

Name _____ *Phone* _____

Address _____

City & State _____ *Zip* _____ *Birthday* _____

Name _____ *Phone* _____

Address _____

City & State _____ *Zip* _____ *Birthday* _____

Name _____ *Phone* _____

Address _____

City & State _____ *Zip* _____ *Birthday* _____

Name _____ *Phone* _____

Address _____

City & State _____ *Zip* _____ *Birthday* _____

Name _____ *Phone* _____

Address _____

City & State _____ *Zip* _____ *Birthday* _____

Name _____ *Phone* _____

Address _____

City & State _____ *Zip* _____ *Birthday* _____

Name _____ *Phone* _____

Address _____

City & State _____ *Zip* _____ *Birthday* _____

Name _____ *Phone* _____

Address _____

City & State _____ *Zip* _____ *Birthday* _____

Name _____ *Phone* _____
Address _____
City & State _____ *Zip* _____ *Birthday* _____

Name _____ *Phone* _____
Address _____
City & State _____ *Zip* _____ *Birthday* _____

Name _____ *Phone* _____
Address _____
City & State _____ *Zip* _____ *Birthday* _____

Name _____ *Phone* _____
Address _____
City & State _____ *Zip* _____ *Birthday* _____

Name _____ *Phone* _____
Address _____
City & State _____ *Zip* _____ *Birthday* _____

Name _____ *Phone* _____
Address _____
City & State _____ *Zip* _____ *Birthday* _____

Name _____ *Phone* _____
Address _____
City & State _____ *Zip* _____ *Birthday* _____

Name _____ *Phone* _____
Address _____
City & State _____ *Zip* _____ *Birthday* _____

Name		Phone	
Address			
City & State	Zip	Birthday	

Name		Phone	
Address			
City & State	Zip	Birthday	

Name		Phone	
Address			
City & State	Zip	Birthday	

Name		Phone	
Address			
City & State	Zip	Birthday	

Name		Phone	
Address			
City & State	Zip	Birthday	

Name		Phone	
Address			
City & State	Zip	Birthday	

Name		Phone	
Address			
City & State	Zip	Birthday	

Name		Phone	
Address			
City & State	Zip	Birthday	